Roots of Faith in Australia

Salvado, Ullathorne, Polding

Marion Sitzmann, O.S.B.

ST. BEDE'S PUBLICATIONS
PETERSHAM, MASSACHUSETTS

St. Bede's Publications
P.O. Box 545, Petersham, MA 01366-0545

©1992 Marion Sitzmann, O.S.B.

Cover calligraphy and illustrations by Kate Pennisi.

LIBRARY OF CONGRESS CATALOGUING-IN-PUBLICATION DATA
Sitzmann, Marion.
    Roots of faith in Australia / Marion Sitzmann.
        p. cm.
    Includes bibliographical references.
    ISBN 1-879007-06-1
    1. Catholic Church—Australia—Bishops—Biography. 2. Catholic
Church—Australia—History—19th century. 3. Salvado, Rosendo,
1814-1900. 4. Polding, John Bede, 1794-1877. 5. Ullathorne, William
Bernhard, 1806-1888. 6. Missionaries—Australia—Biography. 7.
Missionaries—England—Biography. 8. Missionaries—Spain—
Biography. 9. Australia—Church history—19th century. 10. Catholic
Church—Missions—Australia. I. Title.
BX4696.S58   1994
282'.092'294--dc20
[B]   94-9705
                                                                                      CIP

Contents

Preface

In 1988 Australia celebrated its two-hundredth anniversary as a nation. The first known inhabitants of this now great nation were ice-age aborigines. For thousands and thousands of years, the continent was theirs alone, free of European incursion. In 1642, Abel Tasman became the first European to make contact with the continent. Soon the floodgates to Europe were opened and, eventually, in 1770, Australia was claimed for England by the sea captain James Cook. By 1859 six separate colonies, all ruled by England, had been established. The first permanent settlers, however, were convicts exiled as prisoners, who sailed to the continent in the period from 1830-1877. Truly, a rich historical panorama had been unveiled.

But against an historical panorama sketched crudely here, an equally rich religious theme was being etched upon it. That theme has its beginnings in the selfless work of a trio of Benedictine monks who came to care both for the Aborigines and the convicts. It is their story that I attempt to relate in this book. Salvado worked with the aborigines in Western Australia while Ullathorne found his mission with the convicts of Eastern Australia. Polding, the last of the trio, became the first bishop appointed to Australia. The roots of the Roman Catholic faith were planted by these great men, men whose names loom large as one looks back in time at the interplay of powerful historical forces and equally committed men of faith who helped to shape those forces.

My interest in the religious history of Australia was kindled during a sabbatical granted me by Creighton University, a leave that wound its way to the monastery at New Norcia. There I uncovered the fascinating tales of the religious history of this great country. In the archives of the Benedictine monastic library, I traced the roots of Catholicism to three of these committed men of faith: Salvado, Ullathorne, and Polding.

In completing this monograph I incurred many debts, particularly to the following men and women: to the Jesuits of Creighton University, for granting me a sabbatical leave; to Kate Pennisi for her art work, itself a statement of faith; to Abbot Theodore Wolff for the calligraphy; to Reloy Garcia for proofreading the manuscript; to Dr. Michael Lawler, Dean of the graduate school at Creighton University; to the monks of New Norcia; and finally, to Jackie Masker, who typed the manuscript.

DEDICATED TO:
Fr. Robert Halter, O.S.B.
Mentor/Colleague

Salvado's Missionary Endeavors for the Social Outcasts of Early Australia: The Aborigines

In 1977, E. J. Storman, S.J. edited and published in English for the first time Rosendo Salvado's 1851 report to the Society for the Propagation of the Faith titled: *Memorie Storiche dell' Australia*. Normally, such reports are somewhat prosaic and uninteresting, but Salvado's is exciting as he related the development of the Benedictine Mission in Western Australia, the description of the aborigine natives,[1] points about Australia's natural history, and finally the early colonization of Australia.

Although Salvado is one of the most renowned Benedictine missionaries, no review of his life or achievements has appeared in recent years. This account will help to rekindle interest in this important figure in Benedictine history by: 1) outlining Salvado's life; 2) listing his contributions as a missionary to the aborigines; and 3) suggesting directions for future research in Salvado studies.

But who is Rosendo Salvado? Salvado was Australia's most famous Spanish Benedictine missionary.[2] What Junipero Serra was to the Indians in the western United States, Salvado was to the neglected aborigines in Western Australia. He was born on March 1, 1814, in Tuy, Spain, a Spanish border town near northern Portugal. A statue of the missionary stands in the center of town and one of the streets still bears his name.[3] On March 2, 1814, Salvado was baptized; he was given the name of Rosendo, a name which proved prophetic of his future vocation since he was named after Rudesindus, a Benedictine monk who founded the monastery of Celanovo in Spain.

There was no Benedictine monastery in Tuy, but monks from St. Martin's in Santiago de Compostela often came to preach in the cathedral. Perhaps it was one of these monks who inspired or encouraged Salvado in his vocation. Whatever be the case, at the age of fifteen, Salvado decided to join the monastery of St. Martin's which had one hundred and eighteen members at the time of his entry. The monastery was renowned for scholarship; it belonged to the Congregation of Valladolid, which numbered forty abbeys at the time of the suppression of Spanish monasteries in 1835.

Little is known of Salvado's early years at St. Martin's. In 1830, his religious superiors arranged for him to study music under Padre Juan Copa, one of Spain's most famous organists. When Salvado returned to his monastery of St. Martin's in 1832, he played the organ and continued his studies for the priesthood.

In 1835, there was a major political uprising throughout Spain which resulted in the suppression of all religious communities and the subsequent sale of all their property to reduce the public debt. The suppression of the monasteries and convents left many religious homeless, but Salvado and his brother Santos returned to their family home to live. After spending three years in Tuy working in his father's business, Salvado was contacted by a former confrere from St. Martin's, José Serra, who was now a member of the monastic community of Cava near Naples. Serra received permission to invite Salvado to the monastery of Cava. On September 9, 1838, Salvado left his home for Naples. When Salvado arrived at the monastery of Cava, Serra received permission to privately tutor him in theology, preparing him for his ordination five months later. Immediately after his ordination, Salvado was sent to Rome for more studies at the monastery of St. Callisto. Returning to Cava after his studies, he taught music to the young novices and played the organ for ceremonies in the monastic church.

One day while taking a stroll in the woods near the monastery, Salvado broached the subject of being a foreign missionary to his friend Serra. Soon both monks were inspired to consecrate their lives to the foreign missions; subsequently, they traveled to Rome with permission of their superior to consult with Monsignor Brunelli, Secretary of Propaganda Fide, about their plans to work in the foreign missions. On January 14, 1845, Brunelli informed them they would be sent as missionaries to Australia. As if by accident, John Brady, the newly-to-be consecrated bishop of Western Australia was visiting Rome at the time, recruiting priests to work in the missions.[4] Monsignor Brunelli assigned Salvado and Serra to accompany Brady to Australia. Before leaving Rome, the two Spanish monks were invited to the Vatican for an audience with Pope Gregory XVI, a Benedictine monk himself. His inspiring words to the two young monks were: "Remember that you are sons of St. Benedict, our

great founder. Remember all those Apostles who were
brothers, who converted whole peoples and nations to
the faith, and educated them in the ways of civilized life.
Remember that you are setting out on the same road as
was trodden by them."[5] In addition to twenty-five other
missionaries, Brady, Salvado, and Serra sailed from
London to Western Australia on September 16, 1845,
landing in Fremantle, Australia, on January 8, 1846.

When Salvado stepped ashore at Fremantle in Western
Australia,[6] clad in his Benedictine habit, he was thirty-two
years old. He was short in stature, with dark hair, and a
thick, black, untrimmed beard. His eyes were large, and
he gave the impression of being a strong, determined
man. Despite his brave outward appearance, he had a
cheerful disposition. Physically he was strong and well-
equipped for the tough missionary work he would
undertake.[7]

It was in Fremantle that Salvado and Serra first encountered the aborigines, the native people they were sent to
evangelize. The monks were appalled when they found
some natives wandering in the streets in search of food
and a dozen others guarded by soldiers before being
transported to Rottnest Prison, an island prison twelve
miles west of Fremantle. On January 9, 1846, the day after
landing, the missionary group of twenty-eight sailed up
the Swan River to Perth, arriving in the late afternoon.
Immediately, the party went to the church that was built
by Brady. It was a skeleton of a shack only thirty feet long
and fifteen feet wide with window spaces, but no win-
dows, nor did it have a ceiling. Upon entering the church,
Salvado intoned the *Te Deum*, officially beginning their
lives as missionaries.

Within a few days, Bishop Brady organized three missions for the evangelization of the natives; he then dis-

patched groups of missionaries to the southern and
northern regions, but these failed to secure a footing and
had to be abandoned. The priest who headed the southern mission, Father Thiersé, soon became worn out from
exhaustion; he finally left Western Australia for good in
1846. The missionaries who were sent to the northern
mission were drowned in the waters of the Torres Strait
with only the captain and an Italian priest, Angelo Confalonieri, escaping the sea disaster. Later Confalonieri built a
small hut in the bush, but was stricken by illness in 1848
and died.

On February 16, 1846, in the middle of an Australian
summer, Salvado, Serra, and their companion set out to
evangelize the central region. The entire population of
Perth came out to the edge of the city to see them off,
believing it would be the last time to see them alive.[8] The
main problem that the missionaries encountered on the
first leg of their journey was the fine sand that bogged
down the feet of the oxen and the wheels of the wagons.
At a certain point, the drivers of the wagons refused to go
any further; they dumped all the belongings of the missionaries under a eucalyptus tree and proceeded to return
to Perth. Undaunted by these irritating experiences, the
missionaries set about building a hut from the bark and
limbs of trees. No sooner had they finished the hut, when
a group of aborigines approached them with spears.
Unshaken by the fierce-looking natives, the monks proceeded to build a fire and chant the Divine Office. The
next day, the monks set up an altar under the watchful
eyes of the natives who departed at sunrise, but returned
later with reinforcements. After a great deal of coaxing,
the natives finally tasted Salvado's bits of rice cakes and
sugar; they spit them out at first, but then devoured the
sweets like hungry children. In response to the monks'
kindness the natives shared such foods as kangaroos,

lizards, grubs, and wild berries with them. This type of food, however, caused sickness since the monks and their companions were not accustomed to such a diet.

By trial and error, Salvado soon discovered that he could not evangelize the aborigines by wandering around with them in the bush. To this end, Salvado determined to build a monastery, laying the cornerstone on March 1, 1847. The new foundation was called Nova Nursia (now New Norcia) in honor of the birthplace of St. Benedict in Italy. The new monastic foundation was plagued with financial problems. To solve these exigencies, Salvado put on a piano concert in Perth to collect funds. Salvado's plan paid off; he played classical music for three hours dressed in his soiled Benedictine habit and hole-ridden shoes. The seventy people who attended not only felt sorry for him, but were impressed with his abilities as a musician. With the proceeds from the recital, he was able to buy supplies and implements needed for the mission.[9]

As soon as a portion of the monastery was built, he encouraged the natives to live on small plots of land on which cottages were erected and where they could learn the art of farming by growing their own crops. Salvado himself planted the first crops after felling the trees and plowing the desert with a team of bullocks. Salvado's early success as a missionary lay in his policy of making the natives agriculturists first, and Christians second. Later Salvado also set up workshops, forges, mills, and granaries where the natives could work under the supervision of the religious brothers. A writer describes New Norcia settlement almost in terms of a medieval town.

> The present aspect of the Benedictine Village, [New Norcia] like that of many a European City in its early days, is that of a flourishing industrial and agricultural settlement, grouped round the monastery as its center. The latter with its church,

schools, hospital, and guest house, is flanked by workshops,
forges, mills, and granaries, while the cottages of the native
settler, to the number of about fifty, are sprinkled irregularly
over the slope. The daily routine of life in the monastic
settlement is of patriarchal simplicity. It begins at break of
day, when the inhabitants, after prayers in the church, scatter
over the fields in the fulfillment of their various tasks.[10]

Salvado showed great psychological understanding of
the native children in his outline of the daily routine of
school; he stressed the practical arts of sewing, spinning
or cooking for the girls, and light agricultural tasks for the
boys more than the theoretical knowledge of reading,
writing and arithmetic.[11] Reason: the attention-span of the
natives was short. Long periods of study were unproduc-
tive and useless. In addition to their instruction, Salvado
encouraged the young men to go off periodically to the
bush for weeks at a time to hunt. These walkabouts were
important for the gradual culturation process of the
natives.[12] Salvado knew that these walkabouts were
important maintenance of everyday aboriginal life, and
therefore could not be eliminated.

In December 1848, Brady sent a letter requesting the
mission's wool-clippings. Since a lay worker was sick,
Salvado drove one of the wagons himself; he took two of
the aboriginal boys with him. Brady was planning to sail
to Europe when Salvado arrived, but at the last minute
changed his mind; he sent Salvado instead. The two
aboriginal boys begged to accompany Salvado. Brady
decided to baptize the boys immediately, giving them the
names they were called at the mission: John Baptist
Dirimera and Francis Xavier Conaci.[13]

Within a month, on January 8, 1849, Salvado sailed to
Europe with the two aboriginal boys, Francis Conaci and
John Dirimera; he introduced them to the King of Naples
and to Pope Pius IX.[14] If Salvado is to be criticized in

regard to his treatment of the natives, it may be in respect
to his use of two native boys as public relations displays,
faintly realizing at the time the detrimental effect it might
have on the lives of the two boys who were susceptible to
the diseases of civilized society.[15] The two boys met with
the same fate as Upumera, a native boy whom Serra had
taken to Rome a year earlier to study at Propaganda
College; they both died. Conaci died in Europe in 1853
and Dirimera died back in Australia in 1855. James Griffin,
in reviewing Stormon's *The Salvado Memoirs,* questions
Salvado's prudence in taking the two native boys to
Europe. "An aboriginal historian may one day think they
(episodes) show a plentiful lack of common sense in the
good Rosendo (Salvado) who may be deemed as responsible for those boys deaths as if he had carelessly exposed
them to whooping cough or infected their mothers, before
the boys were born, with the pox."[16] In response to Griffin's concern, it can be pointed out that when touring in
Europe Salvado changed his plans in order to follow a
physician's advice when one of the two boys became ill.[17]

When Salvado was traveling in Europe with two aboriginal boys, Serra was also in Europe collecting money for
the mission at New Norcia. Salvado was consecrated
Bishop of Port Victoria on August 15, 1848. Brady wanted
a coadjutor bishop for the Diocese of Perth; he requested
Salvado. Rome, however, at the last minute did a turn-
around by appointing Serra as coadjutor of Perth and
Salvado as Bishop of Port Victoria. Salvado was displeased
with the news of his appointment to the episcopacy; he
worried about what would happen to the mission of New
Norcia. At the time of Salvado's consecration on August
15, 1849, the Catholic Church in Western Australia had
three bishops, but only a handful of Catholics.

Salvado remained in Europe until a return to Australia
could be arranged, but before he could return news

arrived that the British had to abandon Port Victoria.
Since there was no bishopric to care for at Port Victoria,
Salvado requested permission from Pope Pius IX to return
to New Norcia. In the meantime, Salvado received news
that Brady had placed all of New Norcia's property in his
own name. Furthermore, as if to add insult to injury,
Brady gave instructions to his Vicar-General, Urquhart, to
evict Serra and the monks from the monastery of New
Norcia. Following Brady's command, Urquhart accompanied by a lawyer drove the monks from the monastery of
New Norcia at gun point.[18]

For three days the monks walked, after being evicted, to
Guilford where Serra rented a house for them to stay in.[19]
Urquhart, in the meantime, took over all the possessions
of New Norcia; he also took Serra to court, claiming the
property of the monastery for the Diocese of Perth. When
the Holy See heard of the machinations of Brady and his
Vicar-General, Brady was deprived of all his priestly
faculties. Furthermore, the Holy See sent a notice to Serra
to expel Brady from his office. But Brady wouldn't leave
easily; he took his grievances to civil court. Finally, Bishop
Polding arrived from Sydney to inform Brady personally
that he must surrender his position as Bishop of Perth
and hand over all Church property.

When Salvado returned to Perth in August of 1853, Serra
was in charge of the diocese. Salvado's only wish at this
time was to return to New Norcia. Serra promised Salvado to accompany him on a visit to New Norcia, but he
kept postponing the trip until October of that same year.
On the day they were scheduled to leave, Serra became ill
and sent Fr. Aragon to accompany Salvado instead.
Salvado sadly wrote of his visit to New Norcia with these
words: "I met only one brother there who had been
entrusted with the management of the farm. The small
church was used as a stable when I arrived. In the book of

baptisms, the record of tobacco was kept. Everything had been taken from the small monastery…nothing, absolutely nothing had been done for the poor natives."[20] What irritated Salvado was Serra's listless attitude toward New Norcia and his action of diverting the supplies (mostly wheat) to the coffers of the Diocese of Perth. Suffering such indignities from Brady in the past and now from Serra was too much for Salvado; he sought, over the next few years, an independent status for foundation of New Norcia that would have nothing to do with the Diocese of Perth.

By 1857, Salvado had assumed permanent residence at New Norcia. Ten years later on January 28, 1867, New Norcia was raised to the dignity of Abbey Nullius Diocese with its own territory of sixteen square miles. Salvado, already a bishop, was appointed New Norcia's abbot for life and all the Benedictine monks in Western Australia were to be subject to him. New Norcia as a Benedictine monastery now began to flourish. For the next forty years, new monastic recruits from Spain continued to join the ranks of the monks of New Norcia.

On November 30, 1899, Salvado left Australia on his last voyage; he died on December 29, 1900, in Rome at St. Paul's-Outside-the Walls. The account of his death reveals a deep warmth for the aborigines.

> The sickness was short. He (Salvado) received the last sacraments and became feverish. The whole story of his Australian foundation seemed to have unfolded before him. He kept calling by their names the native children of his far away New Norcia, moving his hands and fingers as in the attitude of fondling their curly heads. On the 29th of December, which was the last day of his life, his face lit up and with that strong voice which never failed him, he began to sing the *Salve Regina*. Thus he died with the same prayerful words of

salutation on his lips which he had uttered when he first landed in Western Australia fifty-four years before.[21]

The native aborigines in New Norcia reacted in an emotional way when they heard of the death of Salvado; they wandered for days around the hills as if demented. Three years later, Abbot Fulgentius Torres, who was elected on October 2, 1902, to succeed Salvado, secretly smuggled the mortal remains of Salvado out of Italy on a ship sailing to Fremantle. This procedure was done because of the strict Italian law regarding the transferal of mortal remains.[22] A white marble mausoleum, carved in Genoa, was later placed over the tomb. The tomb with a life-sized bust of Salvado carved on the covering slab is located in the middle of the abbey church at New Norcia.

Three years after Salvado's death, the *Year Book of Western Australia* for 1903 listed the statistics of one hundred and fifty-eight aborigines lodged, clothed, and educated by the abbey of New Norcia. In terms of Australian history, Salvado stands out as one of its most important pioneers; he is unique as a missionary to the aborigines. Despite the primitiveness of an uncivilized Australian bush, Salvado managed to accomplish two things: 1) to introduce European culture to the aborigines through the monastic way of life; and, 2) to make the aborigines settled agriculturists first and Christians second. Many other missionaries (Protestant and Catholic) attempted to convert the aborigines first and then to teach them agricultural skills, only to meet with failure. Even though Salvado's purpose of the monastery as a Christianizing element for the aborigines has disappeared, his dream of a Benedictine monastic way of life for the monks of New Norcia have not.[23]

Salvado's life and work has gone relatively unexplored in Benedictine scholarship. Research in the future should investigate: (1) charges of ethnocentrism in Salvado's work; (2) Salvado's leadership as an abbot and bishop heading an Abbey Nullius; and (3) if the missionaries following Salvado met with success in adapting his strategy of teaching natives to be farmers first and Christians second. There is a wealth of research materials in the abbey archives at New Norcia to enable scholars to explore these issues in depth.

Notes

[1]Cf. Peter Bishop, *Not Slaves, Not Citizens*, (New York: Crane, Russak & Co. 1973), pp. 1-26, and William Howells, *The Pacific Islanders*, (New York: Charles Scribner's Sons 1973), pp. 113-58, where the authors describe the origins of the aborigines. Although a member of *homo sapiens*, as far as racial classification, scientists cannot fit them into any of the three major subdivisions; they are unique among other world populations. The aborigines are genetically a distinct group of *homo sapiens*. They may have inhabited Australia and Tasmania for 10,000 to 20,000 years. Since the aborigines were not gardeners and Australia provided them with no animals suitable for herding, they lived by food-gathering and hunting in which they were limited by distance from fresh water. By the late eighteenth century they numbered about 300,000.

[2]There is a close connection between the early Colonial Catholic History of Australia and the Benedictine Order. William Ullathorne was the first Vicar General of Australia, John Bede Polding was the first Archbishop of Sydney, and his successor, Roger Vaughn, was the second. All three were Benedictines from Downside Abbey in England.

[3]Cf. George Russo's *The Lord Abbot of the Wilderness* (Melbourne: The Polding Press, 1980), p. 1, where he mentions the street as "Calle del Obispo Salvado."

[4]4Cf. William B. Ullathorne, *From Cabin-Boy to Archbishop* (New York: Benzinger Brothers 1941) pp. 214-15, where Ullathorne discussed the appointment of Brady as Bishop of Western Australia. Evidently, Brady, without any communication or permission of his religious superior, Bishop Polding, sailed for Rome. Once he was in Rome, he presented a report about his mission in Perth and petitioned the Holy

See to elevate his missionary territory to a diocese with a bishop. At the conclusion of his petition, Brady mentioned that Ullathorne would be a good candidate for the bishopric. With the petition before him, Cardinal Franzoni wrote Ullathorne a letter inquiring whether he would accept the bishopric and if he were not interested to give him an opinion of Brady. Although Ullathorne declined Franzoni's offer, he did write a favorable letter praising Brady as a hard-working priest, not dreaming that his letter would be interpreted that Brady was an ideal candidate for the bishopric. As events turned out Brady was appointed as the first bishop of Western Australia Later when Brady bungled everything so badly that he had to leave Western Australia in disgrace, Ullathorne was blamed by the Holy See for his letter of recommendation.

[5]E. J. Stormon, ed. & trans., *The Salvado Memoirs* (Nedlands: University of Australia Press 1977) p. 20.

[6]Western Australia had never really been of interest to the British government either politically or economically. In fact, as late as 1825, the boundary maps of British territory in Australia did not even include Western Australia. Britain was mainly interested in the colonies in Eastern Australia which were rich producers of wool and agricultural products. The city of Perth was the first settlement in Western Australia. Captain James Stirling brought a hundred and fifty immigrants there in 1829.

[7]Russo, p. 24.

[8]Stormon, p. 31.

[9]"Perth Gazette," May 23, 1846.

[10]"The Illustrated Catholic Missions," Vol. 6, No. 68, Dec. 1891, p. 117 .

[11]Cf. *Australia Dictionary of Biography Vol. 2* (Melbourne: University Press) p. 416, where Florence Nightingale confirms that it was in Salvado's school that "grafting of civilizing habits on unreclaimed races was gradually accomplished." See also: "Historical Sketch of New Norcia for Abbot Boniface Wimmer," *Tjurunga* 1976, p. 41, where Salvado is quoted as saying: "Teaching natives how to read, how to write, and arithmetic only, is a great mistake, neither of those things bring the means of a living."

[12]See H. N. Birt's *Benedictine Pioneers in Australia Vol. 2* (London: Herbert & Daniel 1911) p. 484, where he quotes Salvado as to the

purpose of the walkabouts: "By these little excursions I obtain two excellent results—I strengthen the constitution which a too confined life in this generation would undermine, and I teach them by contrast all the advantages of a family life in New Norcia."

[13]Russo, p. 137.

[14]Stormon, p. 98, mentions that Pope Pius IX personally conferred the Benedictine habit on the two boys when Salvado took them with him to an audience with the Pope. "Then turning to the native boys he asked, 'What are these two boys carrying?' 'Holy Father,' I replied, 'each one of these white linen bags contains a monastic habit, and as these two lads are going to become the first Benedictines of Australia, indeed, of a whole fifth of the world, I humbly ask you to let them have the great honor of receiving the habit from your hands.' "I am only too happy to do so,' the Pope replied."

[15]Cf. Russo, p. 138, where he states: "Salvado was shrewd enough to see the publicity value of the boys' presence in Europe. He saw also the human interest aspect when he came to begging for his mission in Western Australia."

[16]James Griffin, "Priest and Piccaninnies: Dom Rosendo at New Norcia, and Elsewhere," *Meajin*, Vol. 36, No. 4, Dec. 1977,, p. 524. Cf. Also C. M. H. Clark's *A History of Australia*, Vol. 3 (Melbourne: University Press), p. 357, where he quotes Florence Nightingale as saying: "Can Europeans civilize aborigines without destroying them?" Clark further points out that the inability to live outside the framework of their own culture was in a sense a blessing in disguise for the aborigines. It prevented the Europeans from using the aborigines for their own purpose and protected them from slavery and forced labor.

[17]Stormon, pp. 95-96. In a personal interview with Fr. Stormon, S.J. in February of 1985 on the subject of Salvado's concern for the personal health of the two aborigine boys who were taken to Europe for schooling, he told me, in support of Salvado's actions, of the incident of Christian Kookina, an abandoned aborigine girl, whom Salvado carried on his back after his oxen and cart were lost in a swollen stream. From evidence contained in letters, Stormon indicated that Salvado told the Sisters of Mercy in Perth not to put any underclothing on the little orphan girl since she was not accustomed to wearing any clothes at all. This advice, according to Stormon, indicates concern on the part of Salvado for culture shock and health of the native aborigines once they were taken out of their indigenous

surroundings. Despite Salvado's solicitude, however, the little girl died anyway in a short time.

[18]Russo, p. 71.

[19]Later Serra diverted all the Spanish missionaries to his own foundation of New Subiaco near Perth. Serra had visions of missions all along the coast of Western Australia. Within two years of its founding, Subiaco failed. Most of the monks transferred back to New Norcia, but this was only after Salvado had once again taken over as abbot.

[20]Eugene Peres, O.S.B., *Dom Salvado's New Norcia: 1846-1900* (Unpublished manuscript) p. 107.

[21]*Ibid.*, p. 336.

[22]*Ibid.*, p.339. Peres mentions that when the remains of Salvado arrived in Fremantle on June 2, 1903, the coffin was "cleverly camou-flaged." Some of the monks at New Norcia told me that the remains of Salvado were shipped in a chest marked "books."

[23]The aboriginal girls' orphanage at New Norcia was closed in 1975 and the Kalamburu Mission which had as many as five monks assigned to it was recently given to the Diocese of Broome. Fewer than ten aborigines still work on the monastic farm and live in homes near the abbey; they have, for the most part, disappeared from the environs of New Norcia.

The Role of Ullathorne
in the Repeal of
Australia's Transportaion Act

One of the most overlooked efforts to remedy the deplorable situation of the convicts in early colonial Australia was Bishop Ullathorne's attempt to repeal the Transportation Act.[1] The Transportation Act of 1718 allowed criminals from Ireland and England to be shipped to the American colonies. The law was supposed to deter criminals and supply the American colonies with labor. When Britain and America went to war in 1776, it was no longer possible to send convicts to the American colonies. Another outlet had to be found. Africa and Canada were considered. but it was eventually decided in 1786 that Australia would be the best place for them.[2] From January 1788 when the first convict ship anchored in Sydney until the last arrived in 1867, some 162,000 convicts were transported to Australia.[3] Once in Australia, the convicts were treated like slaves by landowners. The most incorrigible criminals were detained in jails on Norfolk Island. For years, no one spoke out against the grave injustices of the Transportation Act until the arrival of William Bernard Ullathorne as vicar-apostolic of Australia in 1832; he was concerned with the convict situation from the first day of his arrival in New South Wales.

In order to consider in detail Ullathorne's involvement
in the repeal of Australia's Transportation Act, let us
examine: 1) biographical data on Ullathorne's life, 2)
Ullathorne's call for significant social change, and finally
3) resistance from the establishment. From this outline,
one might be tempted to classify Ullathorne as a social
agitator, but there is nothing that would warrant such a
title except for the fact that he was a lineal descendant of
St. Thomas More who was beheaded for his protest of the
divorce of Henry VIII. Biographically, however, there are
some currents in his life that make him stand out as a man
of strong moral convictions.

Biographical Data on Ulllathorne's Life

William Bernard Ullathorne was born on May 7, 1806, in
Yorkshire, England, the oldest of ten children. When only
thirteen years of age, he asked his parents for permission
to go to sea as an apprentice. For three and a half years,
he sailed the Baltic and Mediterranean, and then decided
to enter St. Gregory's College at Downside as a postulant
for the Benedictine Order. Strangely, at the age of seven-
teen, Ullathorne still had not received his first Com-
munion or Confirmation. On March 12, 1824, he received
the Benedictine habit, being professed as a monk on April
9, 1825, and later ordained to the priesthood in September, 1831.

Shortly after his ordination, Ullathorne agreed to go to
Australia as the first vicar-apostolic. Sailing from England
in the autumn of 1832, he reached Sydney in the spring of
1833, but upon his arrival, much to his surprise, found
only four priests working in the missions. By 1835, Ullathorne was convinced that the Australian mission should
be detached from the Diocese of Mauritius which was

thousands of miles distant from Australia. Rome granted Australia the privilege of being a diocese on its own, and Fr. Bede Polding, O.S.B., Ullathorne's novice master back at Downside Abbey, was appointed the first bishop of Sydney with Ullathorne serving as vicar-general. From his remarks made in his autobiography: *From Cabin Boy to Archbishop,* one can see that Ullathorne was the power behind the episcopal throne in Australia; he was also the one who bore the numerous vicious attacks that were leveled against the Church in Australia.

Leaving Australia for good in 1840, he was nominated to several bishoprics in Australia, but refused them all, becoming instead a parish priest at Coventry in England.[4] Two years later, he was appointed vicar apostolic in charge of the central district in England. In 1848, the English bishops chose Ullathorne as their representative in negotiating with Rome for the restoration of the hierarchy in England. Ullathorne was the last of the vicars apostolic who governed England; he became the first Archbishop of Birmingham in 1850. Cardinal Newman was one of the prominent priests in his diocese. In 1870, Ullathorne attended the first Vatican Council; he was responsible for drafting many sections of the documents. Receiving permission to resign his Birmingham See in 1888, he retired to Oscott College where he died on the Feast of St. Benedict, March 21, 1888. Let us now return to the original outline of this account and examine the writings of Ullathorne.

Ullathorne's Frustration with the Government's Position on Criminals

When Ullathorne arrived in Sydney in the spring of 1833, he was warmly received at the colonial office. Father

Therry, a priest in Sydney who was at odds with the
governor in charge, was suspended from his government
appointment as chaplain. Replacing Therry as chaplain,
Ullathorne was given an official government appointment
with a salary. In spite of being on the government payroll,
Ullathorne soon became disenchanted with the establishment because of the way criminals were treated: "We
have taken a vast portion of God's earth and made it a
cesspool…we have poured down scum upon scum and
dregs upon dregs of off scourings of mankind and we are
building up a nation to be a curse and a plague."[5]

What troubled Ullathorne most was how misinformed
the English and Irish were with regard to the evils of
transportation, the cruelty towards the prisoners, and the
depravity the prisoners had to suffer because of confinement. In *The Horrors of Transportation,* Ullathorne claimed
that the English and Irish were completely misinformed;
they committed crimes to be transported and rejoiced in
court when their fate was announced.[6] The reason why
criminals committed these crimes was because of poverty
and distress; they believed falsely that transportation was
not much more than a separation from friends and country.[7] Ullathorne attempted to disabuse the English and
Irish of these false ideas by citing examples; he was an
eyewitness to the conditions which convicts had to suffer
in Australia, indicating that it was much better to go to
Australia as a free emigrant than as a convict and slave.
Furthermore, the government was offering free passage to
Australia for young married laborers and mechanics. The
convict, however, became the property of his owner, who
fed and clothed him; he was given no wages for his work.
The housing provided by the landowners was no better
than that given to animals.

Furthermore, some of the Irish and English, according to
Ullathorne, also had the mistaken idea that deceased

convicts had left huge sums of money in wills to relatives living back in England and Ireland. Ullathorne hoped to quell these rumors by citing historical facts. When convicts were first sent to New South Wales, there were no free emigrants in Australia. Convicts and those in charge of them were the only inhabitants. Out of necessity, the government had to pardon some so that the colony might be settled. This condition soon changed with the influx of emigrants coming to Australia. The new emigrants wanted as many slave convicts as possible in order to increase their wealth. Now it was rare for a convict to obtain his freedom until his entire sentence was worked out. Many of the former convicts who returned to England or Ireland wanted to save face; they didn't want to cite what indignities they suffered. Letters received from convicts indicated favorable accounts, but many convicts wrote favorable letters out of deference to family members. Some wives, misled by these letters, had gone to Australia to seek out their husbands, only to find them in a chain gang, if they found them at all.

In terms of cruelty shown to the prisoners, Ullathorne described the tortures that could occur on board ship on the voyage to Australia. Flogging was the main punishment for misconduct. At night, a half a dozen criminals had to share one couch, huddling together with no distinction being made as to crime. The murderer was thrown together with the petty thief.[8] Once the ship arrived in Australia, the convict was tossed into the barracks where he suffered monstrous torments and indignities. Each convict carried every little thing he had on his person for fear it might be stolen. Soon the convict was assigned to a master without any distinction once again as to what crime he had committed. The Negro slave was treated better than the criminal by his owner; he had cost a great deal of money, whereas the criminal

came as free labor. The criminal cost only one pound, and
this amount was to pay for the clothes on his back.

The master kept the criminal in line by harassing him as
much as possible. The convict was subject to the caprice
of his master; he was likely to be sent to a chain gang,
scourged for idleness, or for insolent looks, or for anything at all. The punishment meted out, if crimes of
drunkenness, disobedience, neglect or abusive language
were committed, was not only arbitrary, but severe; it
often resulted in being put into chains to work on public
roads. If the crime committed was serious, the criminal
was sentenced by a prejudiced master without any form
of trial or jury. Once condemned, the criminal's hands
were tied, his back scourged, and his feet put into heavy
irons to work on the public roads in the hot, unbearable
Australian sun. If the convict behaved well for the period
of his sentence, his master might recommend him for a
ticket of leave. This recommendation allowed him to earn
wages, but his employer was not bound by law to pay
him. The persuader to work and good order was the lash;
it inflicted horrible torture, frequently leaving the back
bloody and bruised. The scourges were accompanied by
violent screams, and criminals often fainted from the
beatings.

Concerning the depravity the prisoners had to suffer
because of confinement, Ullathorne alludes to homosexuality or buggery, but he never uses either of these words.
Moreover, nothing is mentioned about homosexuality in
any of the reports on convict establishments and transportation until after 1830.[9] When speaking of the crimes of
homosexuality in the prisons before the Molesworth
Committee. Ullathorne refers to them as "crimes that, dare
I describe them, would make your blood freeze and your
hair rise erect in horror upon the pale face."[10] Robert
Hughes implies that in Ullathorne's testimony before the

Molesworth Committee the priest hints at more than he can openly tell:

> Few of them had any homosexual experience before they got to Australia, according to Ullathorne, and his testimony was more than guesswork, since as a priest he had heard thousands of prison confessions and had to struggle with his conscience; he testified, generalizing so as not to violate the seal of the confessional.[11]

Others, too, have commented that giving testimony to the committee was a special ordeal for Ullathorne because of his fear of accidentally revealing confessional secrets.[12] During the hearings, he whispered with the chairman in private and spoke to the committee with nervous rapidity. "Bishop Ullathorne visiting Norfolk Island in 1835-36, heard at second hand (from a Protestant clergyman, who had been told it by a prisoner under sentence of death) that 'two-thirds of the island were implicated' in homosexual activity."[13]

Ullathorne's Call for Significant Social Change

In 1836, Ullathorne sailed for Europe; he began his campaign to uproot the convict system while on board ship by writing the Catholic *Mission in Australia* to persuade the working classes in England that their condition would not improve by their joining the convict ranks. The pamphlet quickly went through six editions with eighty thousand copies being distributed in French, German, Dutch, and Italian. The success of the work was so immediate that he was urged to write a short tract exposing the convict system in Australia for the benefit of the Irish.

Ullathorne titled his latter work *The Horrors of Transportation*. The thirty-page pamphlet stressed the legal aspects of the convict system and their social consequences. The *Catholic Mission in Australia* analyzed the moral effects of the transportation system on individuals and society. A copy was sent to the Select Committee of the House of Commons, chaired by Sir W. Molesworth, to inquire into the efficacy of the transportation system as a punishment, its influence on the moral state in the colonies, and how far it could be improved. The effectiveness of Ullathorne's two day testimony on February 8 and 12, 1838, is evidenced by the inclusion of lengthy passages of his testimony in the final *Report* which was published, recommending the abolition of transportation.

Resistance from the Establishment

When Ullathorne returned from Europe in December, 1838, he immediately met controversy. The people in Sydney branded him "Very Reverend Agitator General of N.S.W."[14]

> Scarcely had I landed a day, when I found that I was, and for some time had been, the object of universal indignation in the colony, and indeed throughout the other penal settlements. Several chief officials and other leading men had given evidence, and that in language both plain and strong, on evils and vices of the convict system, before Parliament as well as myself; but I had been selected as the scapegoat for all. Others they ironed, me they resolved to skin.[15]

Two points seemed to irritate the Australians: 1) Ullathorne's mention of the depravity of the prisoners, and 2) the fact that the economic base would be destroyed if the transportation system were eliminated. Those who had grown rich on the convict system knew that when the system was abolished, they would face economic crisis.

Sheep stations, farms, trade, and manufacturers were all worked with convict labor. Ullathorne realized the reasons for the uproar: "I had deeply wounded both freemen and emancipists in two ways, had touched them in two most sensitive points, in their pride and in their pockets."[16] More than five hundred people petitioned the Legislative Council of New South Wales to do something to counteract the talk about "Sodom and Gormorrah" and the rising crime rate.[17] The colonists wanted the transportation system to continue; they considered it an economic necessity.

The newspapers were relentless in their condemnation of Ullathorne, not only for his writings against transportation, but also for his oral testimony before the Molesworth Committee: "In due course, Ullathorne's condemnations filtered into the Australian press. His sharp criticism of injustice towards the convicts and of the practice of assigning prisoners to landowners as virtual slaves angered those who were enriching themselves with free labor."[18] To counter the attacks in the public press, Ullathorne launched a campaign to establish a Catholic newspaper, *The Australasian Chronicle*, in August, 1839.

On August 1, 1840, the convict system in Australia ceased; however, it was not feasible to end the system all at once, and so transportation continued to Van Dieman's Land and Norfolk Island until the late 1860s.

In terms of evaluating the social protests of Ullathorne, one might say that his protest arose from a strong dissatisfaction with the government over the transportation law; he felt that he was powerless to do anything about cruelty and moral depravity among the prisoners in colonial Australia, and so he carried his campaign to the seat of power, England. This is why he wrote his pamphlets *The Horrors of Transportation* and *The Catholic Mission in Austra-*

lia, and personally testified before Parliament on the evils of transportation.

Ullathorne would hardly have been successful in his protest if there weren't some widespread sympathy for his ideas. If Ullathorne hadn't written his pamphlets and if he had not been so closely associated with convictism in Australia, it does not seem likely that he would have been invited to testify before Parliament. His pamphlets began a cumulative process towards a position which should have come about anyway, namely the abolition of transportation. Without Ullathorne's pen and voice, society probably would have gone on as usual with a complacent conscience until some other protester emerged to carry the banner.

It is pure speculation, but the reasons why Ullathorne was so successful are due to: 1) the great numbers of Irish Catholics that he appealed to in his pamphlets and speeches, and 2) the fact that he was a Roman Catholic prelate, and 3) the point that he carried on his protest thousands of miles away from the scene of his attackers. Had Ullathorne published his pamphlets in Australia and testified before the colonial government, he would have met with disaster.

As Australia celebrated its two-hundredth anniversary in 1988, it could look with pride to religious leaders like Ullathorne. Throughout Australia today, there are still depressing reminders of the transportation systems in buildings at Port Arthur and Norfolk Island. The proponents of transportation hoped that the system would deter, reform, and colonize the prisoners. In the light of history, one can say that it only accomplished the latter, and has left only a bitter, tarnished memory of a detested past.

Notes

[1]See Robert Hughes *The Fatal Shore* (New York: Alfred A. Knopf 1987) p. 478, where Hughes credits Ullathorne with the distinction of being the chief witness at the inquiry that helped to abolish transportation. "For the Catholic priest was the vicar-general of Australia, William Ullathorne, later to be the chief witness in the inquiry that helped abolish transportation to New South Wales." Furthermore, note the article in the *Australian Encyclopaedia, Vol.* IX (Sydney: Angus & Robertson 1926) p. 70, which states that: "Many historians have overlooked the great influence of Ullathorne on the decision (repeal of the Transportation Act)." See also Cuthbert Butler's *The Life and Times of Bishop Ullathorne* (New York: Benziger Bros., 1926) p. 90, where he mentions that the work of Ullathorne in the abolition of transportation and the whole convict system was "the great achievement of his life."

[2]Hughes, pp. 57-62. The writer distinguishes between the Transportation Act of 1718 which dealt with the American colonies and the new bill of transportation of 1784 pertaining to "places beyond America." The transportation system as carried out in America was totally different from that established in Australia. The American transportation system relied on free settlers who purchased indentured labor. The convicts were sold by middlemen to landowners; they ceased to cost England any money once they were sold. Convicts sent to Australia, however, continued to be an economic drain on England, even though they worked the lands of the propertied class. The English government was totally responsible for the convicts until they gained their freedom.

[3]Ross Terrill, "Australia at 200," *National Geographic*, 173.2 (February, 1988), 217.

[4]See Francis O'Donoghue, *The Bishop of Botany Bay: The Life of John Bede Polding* (Sydney: Angus & Robertson 1982) p. 61, where he states: "Ullathorne received Polding's letter of Good Friday, 1842, telling him that he was appointed [to be] bishop of Adelaide." Ullathorne made a special trip to Rome to refuse the appointment.

[5]5William Ullathorne, *The Catholic Mission in Australia* (Liverpool: Rockliff & Duckworth 1837), p. iv.

[6]Terrill, p. 235, mentions how Matthew Everingham was transported to Australia for such a minor crime as attempting to pawn two

law books; he was only fourteen or fifteen years old at the time and was given a sentence of seven years for the crime.

[7]William Ullathorne, *The Horrors of Transportation* (Dublin: Richard Coyne, 1838), p. 6. A paraphrased summary of the pamplet follows.

[8]See *The Catholic Mission in Australia*, p. 15, where Ullathorne states: "The seven year prisoner crouched with the convict for life...the petty thief with the murderer...the simple countryman with the gaol-polluted felon, and the monster from the hulk."

[9]Hughes, p. 264.

[10]*Ibid.*, p. 266.

[11]*Ibid.*, p. 267.

[12]A. Shaw and C. Clark, eds. *Australian Dictionary of Biography* (Melbourne: University Press) p. 546.

[13]Hughes, p. 271. Perhaps Hughes is a bit prejudiced when he claims that often Ullathorne told the facts about homosexual activities among the prisoners in order to emphasize the moral iniquities of transportation so that he could increase the number of Catholic clergy in Australia. See p. 494, where Hughes states: "Even Bishop Ullathorne had ulterior motives in expounding the horrors of atheism and sodomy Down Under, as he wanted to expand the power of the Catholic mission in Australia."

[14]William Ullathorne, *From Cabin-Boy to Archbishop* (New York: Benziger Bros. 1941), p. 142.

[15]*Ibid.*

[16]Patrick O'Farrell, *The Catholic Church in Australia: A Short History:1788–1977* (Melbourne: Thomas Nelson, 1968) p. 46.

[17]*Ibid.*, p. 47.

[18]Hughes, p. 496.

Archbishop John Bede Polding

The history of the Roman Catholic Church in Australia has its origin with the appointment of John Bede Polding, O.S.B., consecrated as the first bishop of Australia on June 29, 1834. Prior to this, Australia was considered part of the Church in Southern Africa. As with all beginnings, the Church in Australia had a difficult time, given that only seven priests were assigned to this vast continent prior to Polding's landing in Sydney on September 13, 1835.[1] His arrival was made easier due to the presence of William Ullathorne, O.S.B., appointed as Vicar General of Sydney two years earlier. Before his departure from England, Polding had made a request to found a branch of the English Benedictine congregation in Australia; his request was turned down, but with the proviso that he could establish an autonomous Benedictine monastery in his diocese. Even though faced with a population that was partially convict and a wilderness that was extreme, Polding never let his dream of founding a Benedictine monastery and an abbey-diocese in America fade. He no sooner landed on Australian soil than he set about attempting to establish the monastery as his first priority.

Polding was convinced that no good could be done in Australia unless he could see his dream realized.

In order to detail Polding's achievements and failures as the first Archbishop of Sydney, let us examine: 1) his early life; 2) his work with the convicts; 3) his missionary activities; 4) his monastic vision as an organizational pattern for the diocese; 5) his conflicts with the clergy; and 6) his final years.

Polding's Early Life

Polding's birthdate is unknown; he was baptized on November 23, 1774. His parents being dead by the time he was eight, his mother's brother, Bede Brewer, O.S.B., President of the English Benedictine Congregation, supervised his early education. In grammar school, he was educated by the Benedictine nuns near Liverpool; in secondary school he was trained by the monks of St. Gregory's Benedictine College, near Shrewsbury. Even as a young boy his imagination was sparked by the stories of convict ships sailing to Australia. His playmates, noticing his preoccupation with Australia, dubbed him "the Bishop of Botany Bay."[2] He joined the Benedictines at the age of sixteen, taking the name of Bede in deference to his uncle and mentor. In 1814, the Benedictines of St. Gregory's moved to downside near Bath and Polding continued his studies there. Ordained a priest on March 4, 1819, Polding celebrated his first Mass at Downside Abbey. As a young priest, he was striking in appearance:

> He favored long hair. Indeed, he cut quite a figure. His commanding presence, his large blue eyes alive with interest, his deep voice with it deliberate pace (gave credence) to what he had to say. Slender in youth, he gained an appearance of rugged health in these years.[3]

One of his first monastic appointments was as prefect in the school at Downside. In 1824, he became novice master and served in that position until 1826, at which time he was assigned as secretary to the President General of the English Congregation of Benedictines. Having previously declined the See of Madras, Polding accepted the appointment as the first Bishop of Sydney, Australia; he was consecrated on June 29, 1834.

Work with Convicts

Once Polding arrived in Sydney in 1835, William Ullathorne, O.S.B., former novice under Polding and Vicar General of the diocese, informed him of the moral degradation of the convicts being sent to Australia under the provisions of the Transportation Act of 1786. From the beginning, Polding was not only solicitous of the spiritual welfare of the convicts, but for their physical condition as prisoners. As a young monk, Polding was a noted infirmarian, not only for the students and monks of Downside, but for the sick in the neighborhood. Polding made up medicines and ointments, using them in care of sick, a practice he continued even when he was bishop in Australia. He often used his homemade ointments on the cut and bruised backs of convicts who were flogged.

Ullathorne was impressed with the bishop's concern for convicts. Writing in the *Tablet*, he gives a vivid account of Polding's work with them:

> What above all things enkindled his zeal was the state of convict population. Assisted by one or two priests, he raised his altar one day in a goal, another in the convict barracks, another at the penal settlement of Goat Island, another at the great female house of correction, another at the establishment for juvenile convicts. He preached to them, taught them their

catechism, wept over them, heard their confessions from morning to night, then, after all were prepared would some early morning say Mass for them.[4]

Polding worked very closely with the government from whom he received permission to instruct all new convicts who were Catholics. He worked with the convicts when they arrived in shiploads and arranged with the superintendents to keep Catholic convicts at church through a greater portion of the day, giving them instructions in the faith. Sometimes these instructions were done in a visual way by having one of the criminals kneel at his side in the sanctuary of the church, and so instructing all the rest as how to make their confessions. His instructions not only dealt with religion, but with their very conditions as prisoners. He told them how the disciplinary rules would affect them in Australia and how each of them might endure their condition, how each might even shorten his imprisonment.

On August 1, 1840, the Transportation System which sent criminals to Australia was terminated by the English Parliament, but not before over a hundred thousand convicts were sent to Australia. Two indirect influences on its cessation probably were due to Ullathorne's publication of *The Horrors of Transportation*, a pamphlet outlining its social consequences and his two-day testimony before the Molesworth Commission in the House of Commons on February 8th and 12th in 1838.[5] Once the Transportation System came to an end, Polding directed all his energy to missionary endeavors.

Missionary Activities

When Transportation ended, Australia became a land of free men and women. At this juncture, Polding made pastoral concerns the most dominant element in his life, traveling on journeys through the bush on horseback, since there were few roads, to small villages where the people were settling. In a letter to Dr. Brown on January 28, 1839, Polding recounts some of the hardships he had to endure:

> You may judge from this what an active life a missionary in this country has to pass. I ride to Sydney tomorrow...70 miles, and I think no more of it than formerly I did of returning from Bath to Downside, and I shall not be more tired. I live, when I travel, entirely on bread and tea, now and then an egg, nothing more; no wine, nor anything inebriating, and here is the secret...keep the body cool, and you may endure great fatigue without feeling it.[6]

Polding often talked about the missions and missionary zeal with his fellow priests during the time of recreation, evenings at the rectory. He fired their imaginations with stories of missionaries like St. Paul, who trudged from place to place, carrying whatever was necessary for the Sacrifice and Sacraments, always struggling to advance the faith, against all odds.

Shortly after his arrival, Polding emerged as such a zealous missionary that he aroused severe Protestant opposition. The Anglican Bishop, Dr. Broughton, in 1836 openly charged that Roman Catholicism, dangerous and idolatrous, sought the domination and enslavement of all. Sarcastically, Polding answered him with the reply that he didn't think the Protestant religion would have any effect on the religiously abandoned population in the colony.[7]

Polding's missionary efforts with the aborigines, however, were not quite as successful. On the other end of the continent, Bishop Salvado, at New Norcia in Western Australia, was making far more progress. Bishop Salvado was able to devote his entire time to the aboriginals, whereas Polding was responsible for all within his diocese.

Soon, Polding became convinced that he needed more priests as missionaries to travel to the scattered settlements, to instruct the people in their home, and to administer the sacraments. To this end, he sent Ullathorne to Europe to seek help. In Ireland, the bishops received him warmly; he returned to Australia with ten priests. Later in 1842, the Irish bishops established All Hallows Seminary specifically to supply priests for the missions in foreign countries, such as Polding's.

In 1842, Polding decided to sail to Rome to request permission to set up two new dioceses in the colony. His request was answered with the appointment of Robert Willson as Bishop of Hobart in Tasmania and Francis Murphy as Bishop of Adelaide. At the time, Polding was appointed Archbishop of Sydney and Metropolitan for all Australia. The title of "Archbishop" was a break with the past since there were no archbishops in England except in the Anglican Church. Up to this time, Catholic bishops had received the title of "Vicar Apostolic." It was not until 1850 that anyone was given the title of archbishop in England, eight years after Polding received his title. Back in Sydney, Dr. Broughton, the Anglican bishop, protested Polding's appointment, since there were no Anglican archbishops in Australia at this time. In protest, he refused to serve on certain committees with Polding.

At the time, wide faculties were granted to Vicars Apostolic. Polding wanted these privileges to continue. Rome departed from its normal practice, allowing Polding and his suffragans, Willson and Murphy, to have titles to residential sees and at the same time retain all the privileges of vicars general.[8]

With all his missionary activities, Polding had little time to convert Australia along the lines of St. Augustine, founder of Benedictinism in England, by building up a monastery in the heart of Sydney where the glories of religion could be witnessed first hand by the colonists.

Polding's Monastic Vision

Polding's early training as a monk at Downside Abbey in England convinced him that the only answer to Australia's spiritual needs was to set up a series of monasteries in the colony. Australia, he thought, could be evangelized by Benedictine missions centered in an abbey-diocese. The Benedictine missions would act as reservoirs of prayer from where the monks could go out to do the work of God in their missionary territory. The Benedictine vow of poverty could prevent the "accumulation of wealth, the bane of the Church and the destruction of the individual."[9] The recitation of the Benedictine breviary would be the spiritual foundation of the community. The fulfillment of this dream came as early as 1843, Polding wrote to the Archbishop of Dublin:

> My residence has become a monastery. I gave the habit of the Benedictine Order to five on the 24th of August.... My desire is to establish two priests and a lay brother in each mission.[10]

Although Polding obtained a full and formal authorization to proceed with his dream for a monastery and mission territory from Pope Gregory XVI on April 21, 1844, he received only tacit support from his own abbey of

Downside. Polding's dream of founding a monastery, one
sanctioned by Pope Gregory XVI, himself a Benedictine,
did not prove to be practical in the fluid frontier of Australia. Novices, for example, were difficult to find in the
frontier. To solve this problem, Polding endeavored to
recruit all priests of the diocese as Benedictines or, at least,
to serve under a Benedictine superior. Secular priests, not
surprisingly did not take kindly to Polding's monastic
dream. Unfamiliar with monastic thinking, they were
unwilling to be absorbed into a Benedictine community.
They preferred, instead, the life of secular priests, with
their own distinct identity. Then, too, the majority of the
population was Irish, very nationalistic, and consequently
opposed to any English Benedictine rule. That the Benedictines in Australia were English and that their outlook
was that of the landed gentry is clearly revealed in a
rather blatant stereotype of the Irish expressed in a docu-
ment in which Gregory, Polding's Vicar General, refers to
the Irish as "having lesser mental and social habits."[11]

One of the loudest voices of opposition to Polding's
dream came from a diocesan priest, Fr. McEncroe. In
a petition to Pope Pius IX, he initiated an attack that
eventually led to the final collapse of the Benedictine
monastery in Sydney in 1853. McEncroe was upset with
Polding's idea of tithing the state-aid allowances provided
by the colonial government to the Australian clergy.
Polding wanted to use the money from the tithing to
support seminarians who were being trained for the
missions in Australia at All Hallows Seminary in Ireland.
From the time of the founding of All Hallows Seminary,
Polding began to earmark seminarians to work in his
diocese by paying for their tuition. McEncroe was successful in organizing not only the priests in the colony, but
also the laity against Polding's plan of tithing, as well as
against everything that was Benedictine.

Another element leading to the failure of Polding's Benedictine dream was the protest on the part of some of the Order priests who came to Australia to work in the missions. They, too, felt they were being forcibly Benedictinized against their will. The Passionists and Marists were under the assumption they would still enjoy a certain autonomy in establishing houses in the colony, but they were soon disabused of this idea by regulations concerning their work and finances.

Ullathorne, Polding's first Vicar General, saw as early as 1838 that Polding's dream would not work in Australia. He drew his first insight from the fact that the Benedictines from Downside Abbey in England would not send recruits. Secondly, he sensed that there would be future conflicts due to cultural differences:

> I have much confidence in the piety and present good dispositions of all our new missioners, but doubt much whether the missions will work well, all the superiors being English, and all the subjects nearly all Irish.[12]

He decided to leave Australia for good, not because he was upset, but he saw with prophetic clarity how the situation was developing.[13] He came to the conclusion that his presence in Australia might be an obstacle to the mission's advancement.

Polding's Benedictine dream lasted only for a brief period. The morale of the monks began to wane just at the time when their numbers reached the high point of forty-five members. The workload and the colonial conditions themselves may have contributed to the final collapse. Many of the monks were very young when recruited and some had been admitted too easily. Further, Polding himself was partly to blame for the monastic collapse; he took too many trips to distant regions of his diocese, and as a consequence could not care adequately

for the spiritual formation of his monks which was so
necessary to turn his vision into a reality. A diarist at the
time recounts the prophecy echoed earlier by Ullathorne,
in a comment recorded on the Feast of St. Benedictine, in
March of 1854:

> Splendid singing in the choir, but very few persons in the
> church to listen to it. It is very evident from differences in the
> attendance of the people even at the earlier Masses of today
> that St. Patrick holds a place in their affections preeminently
> above that of Saint Benedict; and it may even be gathered
> that the Benedictines in general do not possess much of their
> good will.[14]

Problems With the Clergy

Without doubt, one of the most difficult trips that Polding ever had to undertake was to settle a disciplinary
problem in the diocese of Perth as part of his office as
Metropolitan. The problem involved John Brady, appointed Bishop of Perth in 1845. Brady's first episcopal
residence was a shack only four feet square with no roof.
The only protection he had from the elements of sun and
rain was a umbrella. His bed was a chair. The poverty of
his living conditions and diet reflected also the financial
state of his diocese. By 1849, Brady had become embroiled
in a severe financial crisis, to the point of bankrupting
nearly his entire diocese. To solve the exigency, Brady
tried to coerce his coadjutor, Fr. Serra, O.S.B., to surrender
money that he had previously collected. The dispute grew
so intense that Brady sailed to Rome in 1851 to get the
matter resolved in his favor. But once Pope Pius IX heard
the case, he suspended Brady as Bishop, appointing Fr.
Serra in his place to administer the diocese of Perth. Not
abiding by the Pope's decision in the matter once he

returned to Perth, Brady sought to regain his diocese through a civil suit.

It was at this juncture that the Holy See requested that Polding intervene to settle the matter. To do so, Polding traveled thousands of miles by horseback, suffering intensely from the weather during the coldest time of the year:

> [I traveled] hundreds of miles through a wild uninhabited country, travelling days and nights without meeting with hut or man; at night resting on the wet ground, it being winter time, and storms most fearful; branches broken off and whirling about through the violence of the wind, and tumbling on every side; vast trees torn up by the roots, and large lumps of ice cutting one's face until the blood streamed ... twice was I swept off my poor jaded horse by branches hanging down in the dark, and falling on my back, and yet not hurt.[15]

At Perth, by force of will, Polding forced Brady to kneel in front of his entire congregation on a Sunday morning before Mass, to humbly submit to the Pope's suspension and to Polding's authority as Metropolitan. Even after this humiliation, the problem was not solved. Soon after Polding's return to Sydney, he received a letter from certain Catholic members of the community in Perth requesting Brady's reinstatement as Bishop of Perth. Polding responded by suspending all the signers of the letter. Until death made it a moot issue, Brady, who retired to Ireland, never surrendered the idea that he was still Bishop of Perth.

Another conflict which deeply disturbed Polding involved Robert Willson who was appointed, at the suggestion of Polding, to head the diocese of Hobart in Tasmania. Willson undertook the assignment with the stipulation that two conditions be met: 1) that J. J. Therry, the current vicar general, would be removed from Tasmania before he arrived, 2) that the diocese would be free from debt. When Willson, however, took over his duties as bishop on May 11, 1844, Therry was still in Hobart and the debt in the diocese was bigger than ever. In regards to Therry, Polding did not want to remove him because of the good work he had done as vicar general in the diocese of Hobart. Therry, for his part, refused to surrender any financial accounts or agree to any arbitration.

For fourteen years, the dispute dragged on. During this time, communication between Polding and Willson became more estranged. Willson thought that Polding didn't take any action against Therry because he wanted to keep his friendship alive. He wanted Polding to come to Hobart to settle the matter, but Polding refused to do so. Polding finally convinced Therry to give in, but not before accounts of the dispute were published in newspapers in Sydney, Perth, London, Dublin, and Paris. In 1865, Willson sailed for England, taking documents with him to clear his name; he hoped to show that all the fault in the dispute resided with Therry, but he died the following year in Nottingham before he could achieve his purpose.

Perhaps the dispute that most troubled Polding was raised by the members of St. Mary's Benedictine community. In an interview with Pope Pius IX, Polding was asked to answer two accusations. The first inquiry concerned Fr. Gregory, the vicar general, and the Benedictine administration of the monastery in Sydney. For many years, Polding was caught between the demands of being an administrator and those of being a pastor; he chose the pastoral, leaving the administration to Gregory. But Gregory was disliked by the monks, diocesan priests, and the laity:

He was not a success as vicar general or prior, and probably his personality was one of the great determining factors in the destruction of the Benedictine dream. He was not suited by temperament for government, and antagonized almost every group of Catholic people.[16]

The second accusation concerned the tithing of the state aid allowances, an issue raised by McEncroe in a petition to the Pope. The Irish were strongly opposed to the tithing issue; they didn't want any of their money sent to All Hallows Seminary in Ireland for the education of future priests.

Polding was so hurt by the Pope's inquiries that he offered his resignation, requesting permission to spend the rest of his life in a monastery. The Pope, however, refused to allow him to resign, reassuring him of continued support and confidence. But the encounter with Pope Pius IX left Polding reticent; it turned him off from ever wanting to go to Rome again for a papal audience. From this point on, Polding was convinced that his Benedictine dream would vanish. In the encounter, Gregory didn't fair as well; he was made the scapegoat for all the problems. At the end of 1860, he was recalled to England by the President General of the Benedictines in England on the express orders from the Holy See.

Polding's Final Years

In retrospect, Polding accomplished a great deal in his forty-three years as bishop, archbishop, and metropolitan. Noteworthy was his calling together of the first Catholic Provincial Synod of Australia in 1844, the founding of two Catholic newspapers, and his pastoral letters. In his pastoral letters, his sensitivity to the nuances of colonial life is evident. His seventy pastoral letters cover a variety of subjects: education, hospital, capital punishment, censorship, aboriginals, the role of women, family, and the responsibility to the government. These letters are religious documents; they indicate his strong belief that religion was virtually involved in all human activity of his people. The pastoral letters indicate the changing nature of Roman Catholicism in Australia. In his writing, Polding tried to give the early Catholic Church in Australia a sense of human perfection, outlining those elements in human conduct that were threatening the Church in Australia at that time. He returned again and again to certain themes of charity, compassion, faith, and the evangelical virtues of poverty and generosity in his writing.

If Polding had weaknesses, they were in the areas of indecisiveness and administration. Kindness and humility were his virtues. His idealism was unmatched, especially in terms of his dream of an abbey-diocese. All during his life Polding was a monk at heart. He lived austerely. His room was like a monk's cell with a small bed, chair, table, wardrobe, and a bookcase. His only treasure was his faith and the dream he tried to erect in its service.

In 1865, Polding made his final trip to Rome, requesting that Roger Vaughn, O.S.B. be appointed as coadjutor, a plea not answered until eight years later, in 1873. One of his final wishes in requesting Vaughan was to ensure a continuing Benedictine presence in Australia, holding out to the last that Benedictinism might still be rekindled and his dream be fulfilled. But it was never realized!

Notes

[1]Cf. Patrick Francis Cardinal Moran's *History of the Church in Australia*, (Sydney, 1896) p. 494 where he contrasts the growth of the Church from the time of Polding's arrival until his death. When Polding died, there were five dioceses and 135 priests.

[2]Frances O'Donoghue, *The Bishop of Botany Bay*, (Angus & Robertson Publishers: Sydney, 1982) p. 2.

[3]*Ibid*, p. 3.

[4]*The Tablet*, March 24, 1877.

[5]A. Shaw and C. Clark, eds., *Australian Dictionary of Biography*, (Melbourne: University Press) p. 545. Cf. also my article on "The Role of Ullathorne in the Repeal of Australia's Transportation Act," *American Benedictine Review*, Vol. 40:3, September 1989, pp. 323-332.

[6]H. N. Birt, *Benedictine Pioneers in Australia*, Vol. 1 (Melbourne: University Press) p. 317.

[7]Mary Leavey, *John Polding*, (Oxford University Press, 1972) p. 7.

[8]John Molony, *The Roman Mould of the Australian Catholic Church*, (Melbourne: University Press, 1969) p. 15

[9]Leavey, p. 7.

[10]Birt, p. 66.

[11]T. L. Suttor, *Hierarchy and Democracy in Australia 1788-1870*, (Melbourne: University Press, 1965), p. 77

[12]O'Farrell, p. 43.

[13]*Ibid.*, p. 53. Cf. where O'Farrell offers another reason why Ullathorne decided to leave Australia. Evidently, Polding made it clear that as Vicar General Ullathorne was to bear the brunt of the attacks that came to the episcopal office. At first he was willing to do this, but eventually became a little resentful of the task.

[14]O'Donoghue, p. 83.

[15]Leavey, p. 9.

[16]*Ibid.*, p. 16.